DATE DUE	
DEC 1 8 2011	JAN 0 2 2013	
JAN 1 3 2012		
FEB 2 5 2012		
MAR 2 4 2012		
OCT 0 8 2012		

How Big Were the Dinosaurs?

More books by Bernard Most:

ABC T-Rex
Dinosaur Questions
If the Dinosaurs Came Back
The Littlest Dinosaurs
Whatever Happened to the Dinosaurs?

Cock-a-Doodle-Moo!
The Cow That Went OINK
My Very Own Octopus

How Big Were the Dinosaurs?

Written and illustrated by Bernard Most

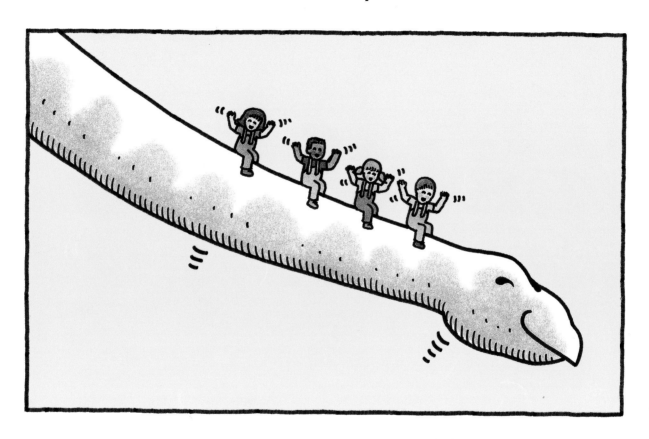

sandpiper

HOUGHTON MIFFLIN HARCOURT

Boston • New York

The Library of Congress has cataloged
the hardcover edition as follows:
Most, Bernard.
How big were the dinosaurs?/by Bernard Most
p. cm.
Summary: Describes the size of different dinosaurs
by comparing them to more familiar objects, such as
a school bus, a trombone, or a bowling alley.
1. Dinosaurs—Size—Juvenile literature.
[1. Dinosaurs—Size.]   I. Title.
QE862.D5M694   1994
567.9'1—dc20   93-19152
ISBN 978-0-15-236800-5
ISBN 978-0-15-200852-9 pb

Printed in Singapore
TWA 25 24 23 22 21 20 19 18 17

The author wishes to acknowledge the following sources
for the factual information contained within the text:
A Field Guide to Dinosaurs by David Lambert
Dinosaur Data Book by David Lambert
The New Illustrated Dinosaur Dictionary by Helen Roney Sattler
Encyclopedia of Dinosaurs, Publication International Ltd.
Dr. Philip Currie of the University of Alberta

To our grandchildren, Samantha, Nicholas, and Jacob

It's hard to imagine how big some of the dinosaurs really were. Some dinosaur footprints that have been found are so big, you and a couple of friends could stand in one of them.

Just how big *were* the dinosaurs?

Tyrannosaurus rex (tie-RAN-a-saw-russ REX) was so big, some of its teeth were as big as your toothbrush, more than 7 inches long.

I wonder how many tubes of toothpaste it would take to brush this monster's teeth?

Triceratops (try-SER-a-tops) was so big, its head was bigger than your front door.

Even though this plant eater was one of the most peaceful dinosaurs, I don't think your mother would want it inside your house.

Shantungosaurus (shan-TOONG-o-saw-russ) was so big, it was about 50 ducks long.

It was one of the biggest duck-billed dinosaurs ever found.

I bet it could make the loudest quack ever!

Stegosaurus (STEG-o-saw-russ) was so big, the plates on its back were larger than a school crossing sign.

With all those protective plates, Stegosaurus would be a perfect crossing guard.

Deinocheirus (dye-na-KYE-russ) was so big, its arms and hands together were 9 feet long. Since that was all scientists ever found of this dinosaur, I wonder how much bigger the rest of it was.

Wouldn't it be nice to have an extra pair of helping hands that size around your house?

Hypselosaurus (HIP-sil-a-saw-russ) was so big, its eggs were the size of a hen. Even though this barn-sized plant eater was smaller than many other dinosaurs, its eggs were some of the biggest dinosaur eggs ever found.

Do you think eggs that big would fit in an egg basket?

Supersaurus (SOO-per-saw-russ) was so big, it was longer than a supermarket aisle.

I bet this gigantic plant eater would have no trouble finding the vegetable section.

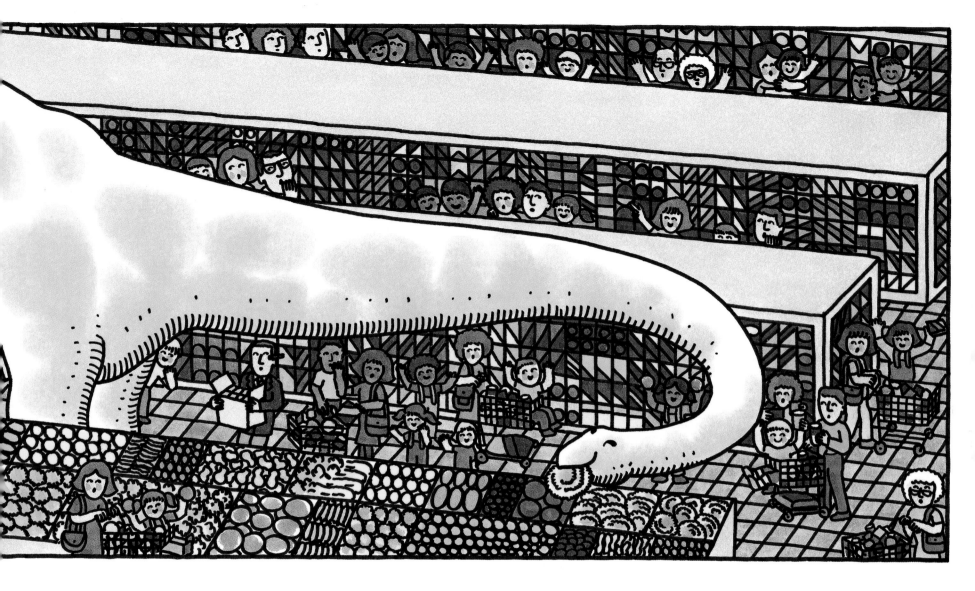

How about calling this dinosaur Supermarketsaurus?

Ankylosaurus (an-KILE-a-saw-russ) was so big, it was bigger than a school bus. This sturdy plant eater was covered with armor and weighed more than 5 tons.

Wouldn't you feel safe going to school on an enormous dinosaur bus?

Allosaurus (AL-a-saw-russ) was so big, it was bigger than a bulldozer. This meat eater's jaws were hinged, so it was able to swallow large chunks of meat. Whenever I see the powerful jaws of an earth-eating machine, I think of Allosaurus.

Apatosaurus (ah-PAT-a-saw-russ) was so big, at 1 month old it was bigger than a baby's crib.

I bet it wasn't easy to babysit a 6-foot-long, 75-pound baby Apatosaurus!

Parasaurolophus (par-a-saw-ROL-a-fuss) was so big, the hollow tube at the top of its head was longer than a trombone. Some scientists think it blew air through this tube to make hornlike sounds.

I wonder how it would have sounded in a school concert?

Diplodocus (dih-PLOD-a-kuss) was so big, it was about as long as a basketball court.

One of the longest dinosaurs ever found, it could have been nicknamed "stretch lizard."

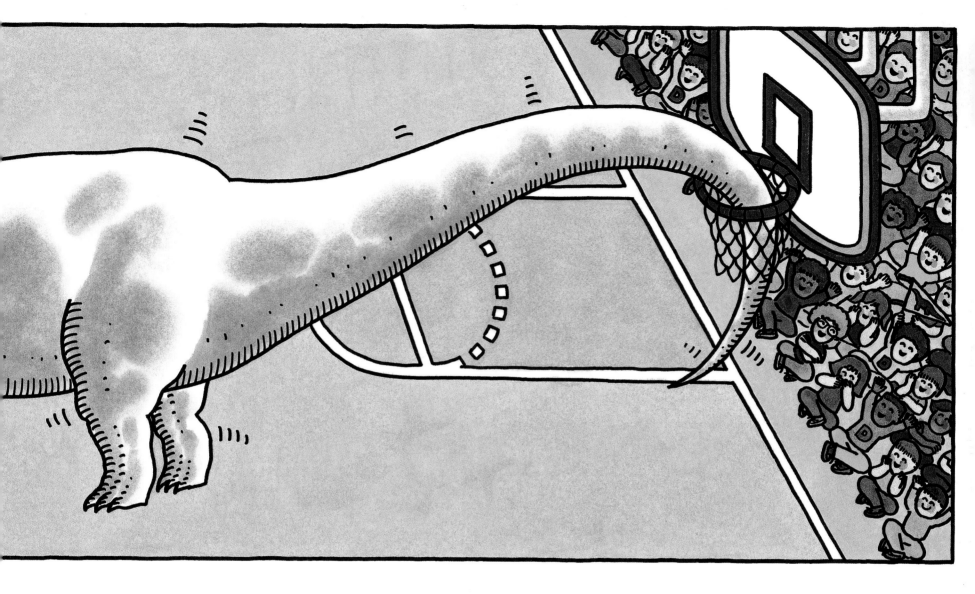

I bet Stretch would have been able to slam-dunk its head and its tail at the same time!

Baryonyx (bar-ee-ON-ix) was so big, its thumb claws were as big as this book. Its nickname was "heavy claw."

Do you think this very large dinosaur would like to thumb through this dinosaur book?

Mamenchisaurus (ma-MEN-chee-saw-russ) was so big, its neck was longer than a school flagpole. No other dinosaur, or any animal that ever lived, had a longer neck.

I think this dinosaur is worth saluting.

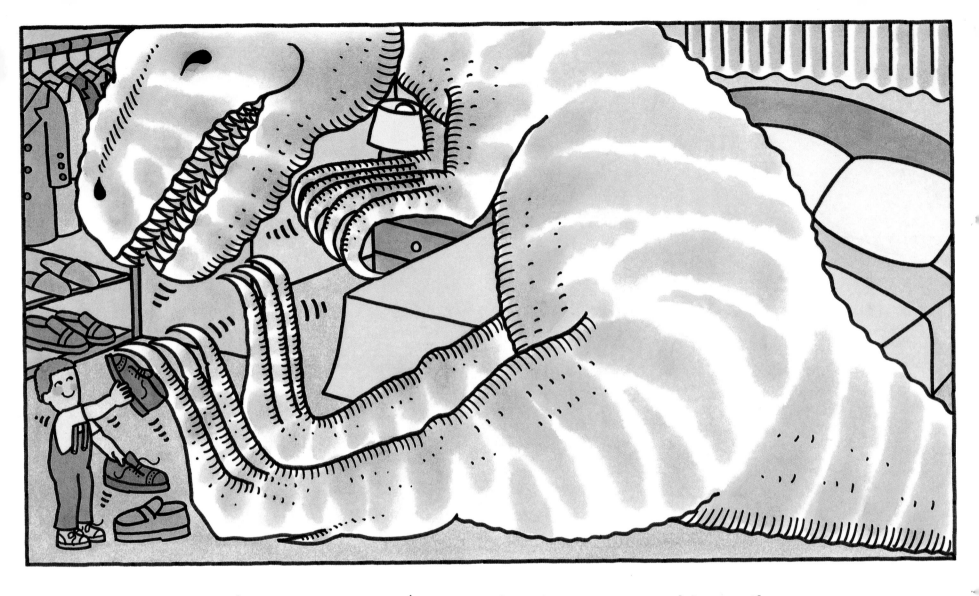

Torvosaurus (TOR-va-saw-russ) was so big, its toes were bigger than a man's shoes. Scientists named this large meat eater "savage lizard" because of the giant claws on its hands and feet.

I bet you thought only grown-ups had big feet!

Brachiosaurus (BRAK-ee-a-saw-russ) was so big, it was taller than a giraffe, the tallest animal living today.

A giraffe might need help from an elephant and a hippopotamus to reach as high as Brachiosaurus.

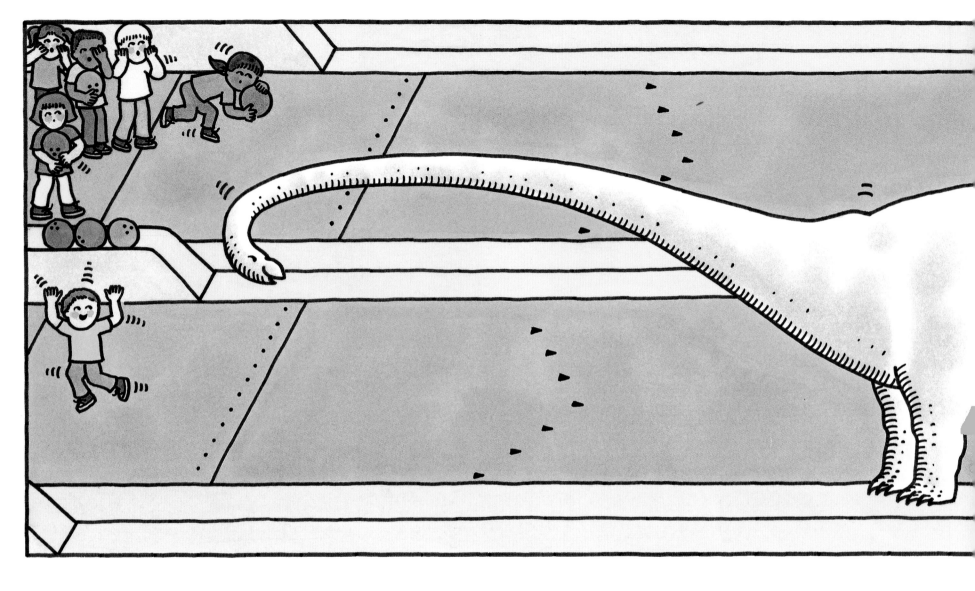

Omeisaurus (o-may-ee-SAW-russ) was so big, it was longer than a bowling alley lane. Scientists think it might have had a bony club at the tip of its tail. It sure would be fun to go bowling with this dinosaur!

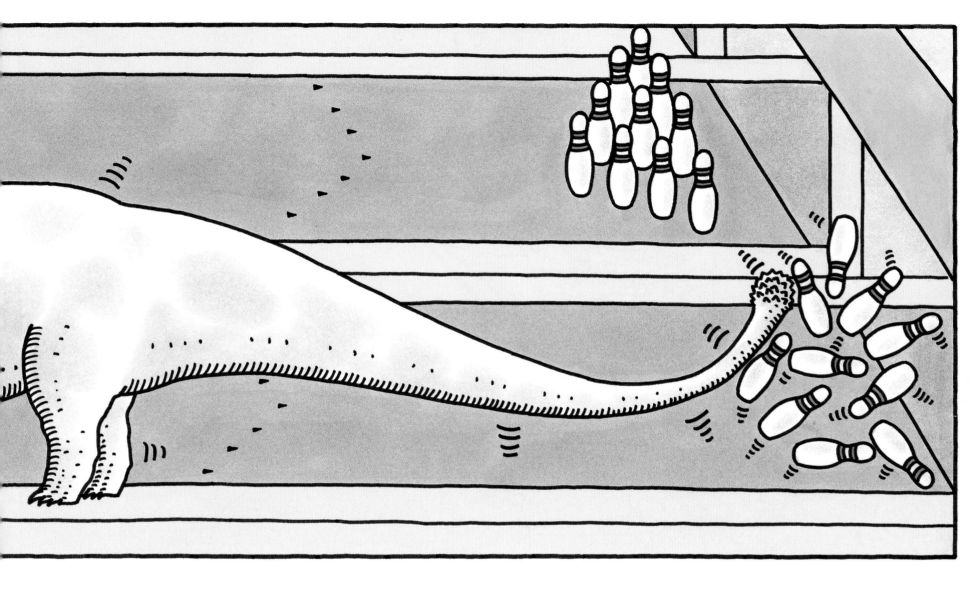

S-T-R-I-I-I-K-E!

Therizinosaurus (ther-ih-zin-o-SAW-russ) was so big, its fingernails were almost as big as you are! Not much else is known about this big-fingered dinosaur.

I wonder how long it would take to polish those huge fingernails?

Ultrasauros (UHL-tra-saw-russ) was so big, its shoulder blade was longer than a park bench.

If just one Ultrasauros bone was this big, imagine how huge the whole dinosaur must have been!

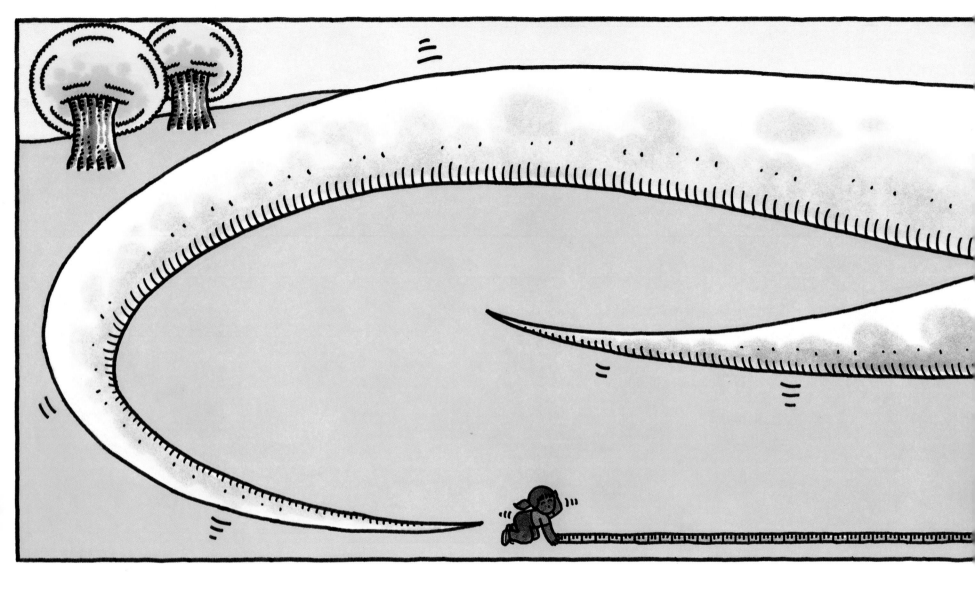

Seismosaurus (size-ma-SAW-russ) was so big, it was almost twice as big and weighed almost twice as much as Apatosaurus, better known as "thunder lizard."

The name Seismosaurus means "earth-shaker lizard."

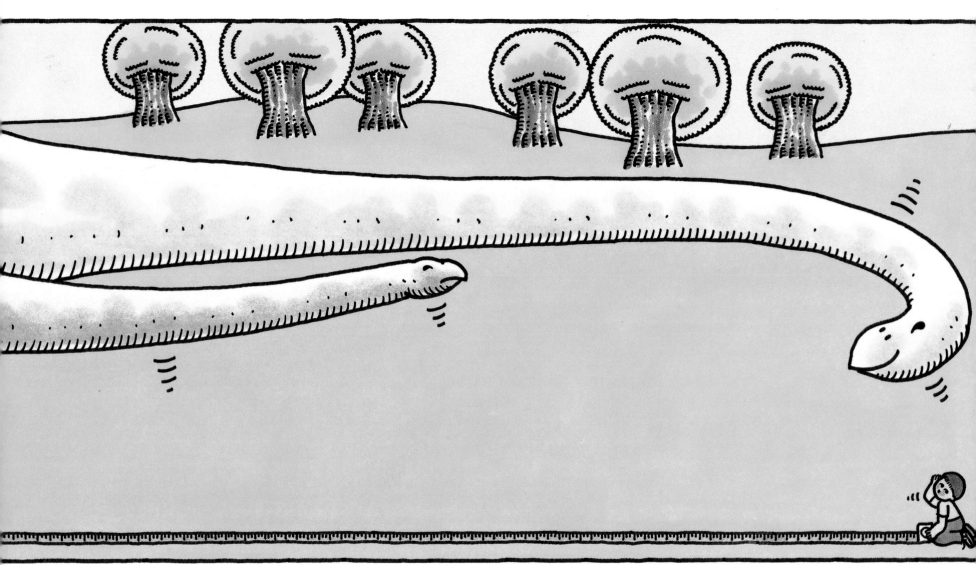

I bet you used to think thunder lizard was big!

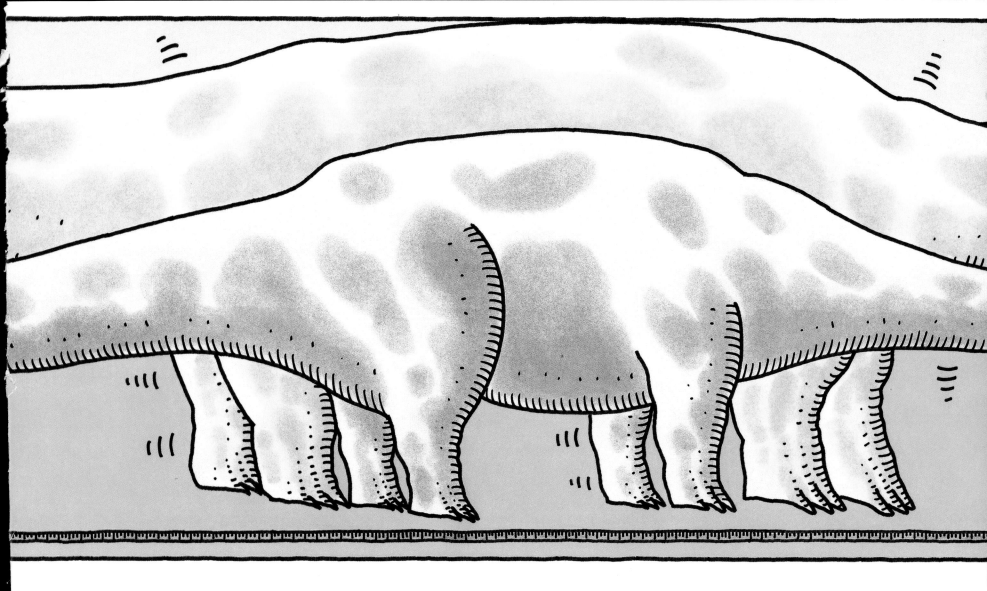

Maybe one day someone will discover a dinosaur so big, it will make "earth-shaker lizard" look tiny!

Omeisaurus
66 feet (20 meters)

Triceratops
30 feet (9 meters)

Shantungosaurus
52 feet (16 meters)

Hypselosaurus
40 feet (12 meters)

Torvosaurus
33 feet (10 meters)

Supersaurus
80–100 feet (24–30 meters)

Ultrasauros
100 feet (30.5 meters)

Parasaurolophus
33 feet (10 meters)

Tyrannosaurus rex
50 feet (15 meters)

Stegosaurus
30 feet (9 meters)

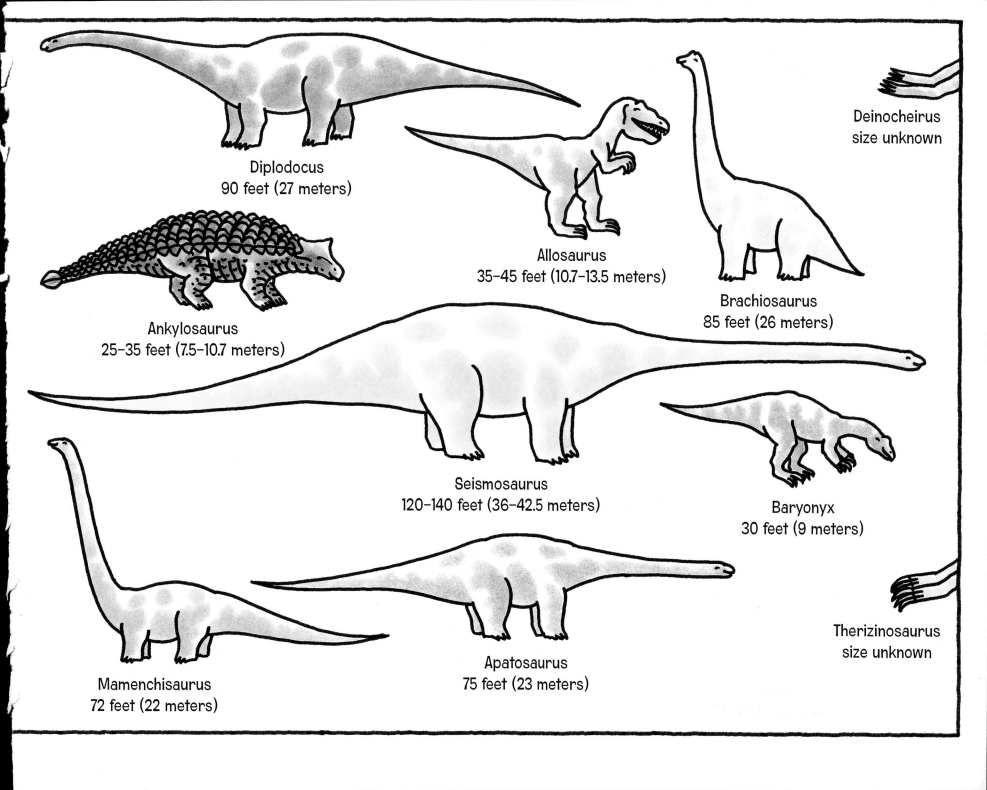

Diplodocus
90 feet (27 meters)

Allosaurus
35–45 feet (10.7–13.5 meters)

Deinocheirus
size unknown

Ankylosaurus
25–35 feet (7.5–10.7 meters)

Brachiosaurus
85 feet (26 meters)

Seismosaurus
120–140 feet (36–42.5 meters)

Baryonyx
30 feet (9 meters)

Mamenchisaurus
72 feet (22 meters)

Apatosaurus
75 feet (23 meters)

Therizinosaurus
size unknown